Aspen King ♡

King

Sibling Love

By

Aspen King

Copyright © 2020 BFF Publishing House, LLC

Printed in the United States of America

Website: www.thejournaljoy.com

Email: Amiyra@thatmommyjoy.com

ISBN: 978-1-7352848-5-9

BFF Publishing House is a Limited Liability Corporation dedicated wholly to the appreciation and publication of children and adults for the advancement of diversification in literature.

For more information on publishing contact

Antionette Mutcherson at
bff@bffpublishinghouse.com
Website: bffpublishinghouse.com
Published in the United States by
BFF Publishing House
Atlanta, Ga. First Edition, 2020

This book is dedicated to my little brother Chandler. Mommy helped me get ready to be a big sister. This book was created to help all families expecting little brothers and sisters.

There is a bump in Momma's tummy!
It's big, round, and moving up and down
We tiptoe up close to listen inside
To our surprise, it sounds like oceans and lullabie

Is it a boy?

Is it a girl?

We just cant tell!

First came Rhea. She's oh so smart! She has Mom's eyes, Dad's curly hair, and she loves to share.

Then came Ryan. He looks like Dad: tall, smart, and always having fun.

Finally! We can't wait to be a party of three!

We will make up songs to help you sleep.

We promise to keep our rooms clean.

Mom and Dad will pick you up.

We will share our favorite toys:

Trucks, trampolines, blocks, and bikes to go on our family hikes.

Rhea brings kisses,
Ryan has high fives.
We promise to get along just for you!
We already love you!

Write down all your promises to your new sibling.

Aspen Serenity King is a dynamic 6 year old, whose gravitating smile and kind personality will light up any room. Aspen developed a love for books as a baby. She looked forward to her daily bedtime stories with mom and dad. As a one year old, Aspen was memorizing books and reciting to mom and dad. At the age 4, Aspen learned how to read. Her love and excitement for books blossomed quickly. Aspen wants to encourage all children to love books as much as she does.

Made in the USA
Columbia, SC
04 December 2020